First published in Great Britain in
2009 and in the USA in 2010 by
Frances Lincoln Children's Books,
4 Torriano Mews,
Torriano Avenue,
London NW5 2RZ
www.franceslincoln.com

British Library Cataloguing in
Publication Data available on
request

ISBN 978-1-84507-981-9

Printed in China

Book design:
Polly Farquharson and Adam Brown.

Thanks to Adam Brown, Ellen
Farquharson, Thomas Neurath and
Howard Sooley for all their help.

for nancy, rose and howard

F

FRANCES LINCOLN
CHILDREN'S BOOKS

The Green Line

a walk in the park

polly farquharson

One sunny spring day,

we went for a walk in the park...

We held hands crossing the road.

We saw flowers peeping
through the fence.

I jumped along the pavement
... jumping on the squares.

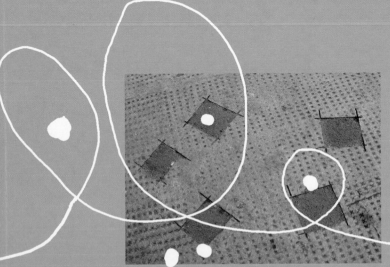

In the park…

I ran and ran
and went roly-poly
all the way
down the hill!

I saw a SNAKE,
so I ran away...
but my mummy said it was just a stick.

Blowy things!

I blew the seeds
away into the sky.

right up to the clouds.

They floated up and up…

I found a little ladybird on a leaf.
        When it saw me it really wanted to
go on my hand.

I saw wobbly raindrops in the grass.

We made a path in the long grass.

A big friendly dog came running up to say hello.

We found hundreds of
buttercups…

and teeny beetles hiding.

It started to rain...
I JUMPED and
SPLASHED and
SPLASHED in the puddles!

We ran through
the rain to a big
umbrella tree.
I heard raindrops
pattering on
the leaves.

When the sun came out

we played   hide

and

seek...

I hid where nobody could see me...

Ssshhh

Along a tickly path…
The flowers were
even taller than me!

We followed fluttery butterflies

... carefully past the stinging nettles!

We lay down
on the grass...

feeling sleepy.

Mummy made me
a daisy chain.

I ran after the pigeons...

and chased them all away!

I found a lovely feather.
I put it in my pocket
to take home.

Fluffy ducklings!

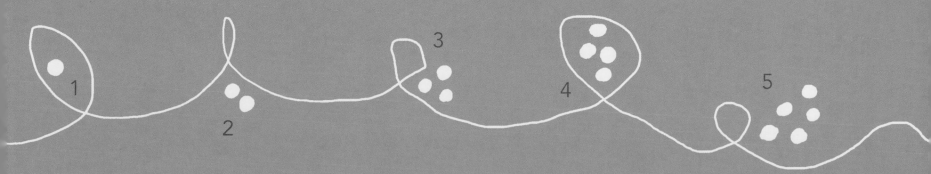

1 2 3 4 5

On the way back we went over the railway bridge.

Mum helped me climb up,
so I could peep
through the window.

I walked on the shadows,
I looked at the reflections

and the clouds followed us...

... all the way home.